ART THERAPy
WORKBOOK
FOR KIDS 9-12

A Fun Guide to Engage your Children to Boost their Emotional Resilience, Improve Behaviour and Social and Communication Skills.

by

Christiana J.

Sellix Publications

ABOUT THE AUTHOR

Christiana J. Ph.D is an experienced professional in the field of Art Therapy for children. With her extensive knowledge and practical experience, she is a highly sought-after speaker and author in the area of child development and mental health. Her passion for art therapy stems from her belief in its ability to enhance emotional resilience, improve behavior, and promote healthy social and communication skills in children. Through her innovative approach, she empowers parents and educators to utilize the power of Art Therapy as a tool for promoting children's mental health and well-being.

With her unwavering commitment to making a difference in the lives of children, Christiana's expertise in the field of art therapy is truly unparalleled. Her work has helped countless children overcome emotional and behavioral challenges, allowing them to develop into confident, resilient, and creative individuals.

CONTENTS

INTRODUCTION

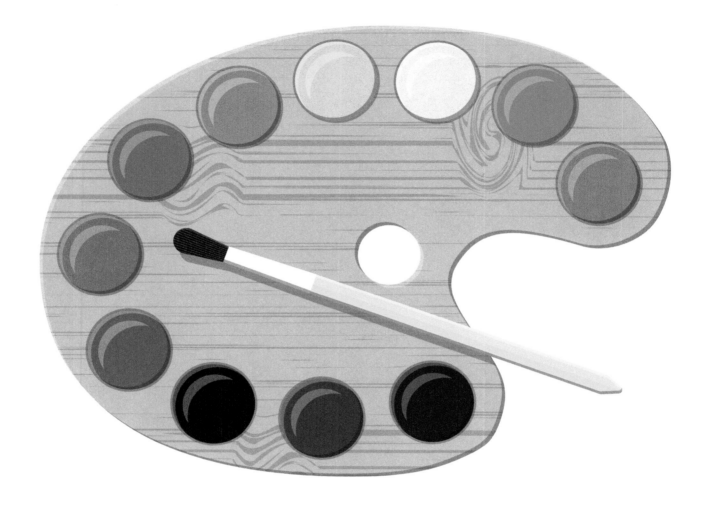

Art therapy harnesses the imaginative procedure of crafting artwork to encourage the articulation, comprehension, and recuperation of emotions.

By means of art therapy, people have the opportunity to delve into their innermost selves, heighten self-awareness, and attain understanding of their feelings and actions

The practice of art therapy promotes personal development, nurtures resilience, and enhances overall mental and emotional health.

Sophie was a 10-year-old girl who had always been shy and reserved. She had a hard time expressing her emotions and often struggled to make friends at school. Her parents noticed her struggles and wanted to find a way to help her build her confidence and connect with others.

It was resolved to attempt art therapy as a means for Sophie to creatively communicate her feelings and investigate her emotions within a secure and encouraging milieu.

They set up a small art studio in their home, stocked with all kinds of art supplies, and encouraged Sophie to spend time there every day.

At first, Sophie was hesitant and unsure of what to do. But as she experimented with different materials and techniques, she began to discover a passion for drawing and painting. She created vibrant, colorful pieces that were full of emotion and energy.

Through art, Sophie was able to express the feelings she had always kept bottled up inside. She began to open up to her parents about her worries and fears, and they were able to offer her the support and guidance she needed. She even started to share her artwork with her classmates, and found that it helped her make new friends.

Over time, Sophie's confidence grew, and she became more comfortable in social situations. Art had evolved into a medium for her to bond with others and convey herself in a manner that seemed genuine and faithful to her identity. Her parents were astonished by the metamorphosis they witnessed in their offspring and appreciated the efficacy of art therapy in aiding their child's recovery and advancement.

Have you ever wondered how art therapy works for children? Although it may seem similar to play therapy, Art therapy encompasses the utilization of diverse art supplies and methodologies to stimulate the fabrication of a palpable outcome that visually represents a child's encounters, viewpoints, sentiments, and creativity. Art therapists employ their proficiency in artistic tools and innovative methods to assist children in expressing and dealing with emotions, ideas, and conduct. By engaging in art-making, children can improve their communication, cognitive functioning, emotional regulation, social skills, physical abilities, and trauma processing. Art therapy also shares similarities with traditional therapy, such as assessment, rapport building, treatment planning, and documenting progress.

Art therapy can be a powerful tool for parents to help their children build emotional resilience, improve behavior, and develop social and communication skills. By participating in different art undertakings, kids can acquire the ability to articulate their emotions in a secure and imaginative fashion. This may result in greater self-consciousness and enhanced comprehension of their sentiments, as well as improved coping techniques for handling stress and challenging circumstances. Art therapy can also foster positive behavior changes by encouraging children to think outside the box and explore different perspectives. Furthermore, the social and communication skills developed through art therapy can translate into improved relationships with peers and adults alike. As a fun and engaging guide, parents can use art therapy to help their children unlock their full potential and thrive both emotionally and socially.

As you hold this book in your hands, you are embarking on a journey to explore the wonderful world of art therapy with your child. This fun and interactive guide is designed to engage your children and help them boost their emotional resilience, improve their behavior, and enhance their social and communication skills through the power of art.

The activities and exercises in this book have been carefully curated to spark your child's creativity and imagination, while also helping them express their emotions and feelings in a safe and supportive environment. By engaging in these art therapy techniques, your child will not only have fun, but they will also learn important skills that will serve them well throughout their lives.

So get ready to dive into the world of art therapy with your child and watch as they develop greater emotional awareness, self-confidence, and self-expression. Together, let's explore the power of art to promote healing and growth, and have some fun along the way!

CHAPTER 1: THE POWER OF ART THERAPY

Art therapy is a form of treatment for children and adolescents who may be experiencing emotional or behavioral difficulties. It involves using different art materials to create art, which can help children express their thoughts and feelings in a non-verbal way. The art-making process is done in a safe and supportive environment with the guidance of a trained professional. The resulting artwork can help children gain insight into their emotions,

develop coping skills, and reduce stress and anxiety. Art therapy has the potential to serve as a valuable mechanism for children and parents to collaborate towards enhancing their holistic welfare.

1.1 UNDERSTANDING ART THERAPY: HOW IT WORKS AND WHY IT'S IMPORTANT

The practice of art therapy involves utilizing creative techniques to enhance a person's mental, physical, and emotional health. By utilizing various art materials, including but not limited to paints, clay, and markers individuals can create artwork under the guidance of a professional art therapist. This form of therapy is aimed at improving overall well-being and can serve as a means of expression and self-discovery.

The act of producing art can facilitate individuals to delve into and communicate their emotions, diminish stress and anxiety, and enhance their self-worth and communication abilities. Art therapy is frequently employed in managing various mental health problems such as depression, anxiety, and traumatic experiences.

Art therapy is a type of therapy that employs the creation of artwork to enhance the psychological and emotional wellness of individuals. It involves using various art mediums such as painting, drawing, sculpting, and even music and drama to facilitate self-expression and exploration. By means of producing art and the direction of a qualified therapist, individuals can acquire comprehension into their emotions, ideas, and conduct. Art therapy has the potential to be efficacious in addressing an extensive assortment of mental health challenges, encompassing trauma, nervousness, despondency, and conduct-related predicaments. It can help individuals to develop coping skills, increase self-awareness, and improve communication and social skills. Art therapy is also used in some cases to aid in physical rehabilitation and pain management.

Art therapists use a variety of techniques and mediums to meet the unique needs and goals of each individual. They may engage in activities such as visual art, movement, music, and writing to help clients express themselves and process their emotions. The therapist will also work to build a trusting relationship with the client and develop a treatment plan that addresses their specific concerns.

1.2 BENEFITS OF ART THERAPY FOR KIDS: ENHANCING EMOTIONAL RESILIENCE, COMMUNICATION AND BEHAVIORAL SKILLS

Children's emotional stability, communication, and behavioral skills have all been found to improve with art therapy. Children can express their emotions in a secure and non-threatening way through art-making. This can aid in the development of emotional resilience, or the capacity to recover from trying situations. Creating art can serve as a beneficial tool for children to process and communicate their emotions. By engaging in art-making, children can develop a sense of agency over their emotions, which can lead to increased feelings of self-worth and assurance. Art therapy can improve communication skills by giving children

a non-threatening and non-verbal way to express themselves. Artistic manifestation is a type of communication that does not involve verbal language, and can function as a potent mechanism for self-expression, particularly for children who may encounter challenges in articulating their thoughts or emotions. Art therapy can also help children learn to identify and regulate their emotions so they can better relate to others.

Art therapy can help children develop their behavioral skills in several ways.

- First, art therapy can provide children with a safe, structured space to explore and express their feelings. This can help them learn to regulate their emotions and behavior in healthy ways. For example, a child who is prone to tantrums can learn to use art as a safe and constructive way to vent their feelings without resentment.

- Second, art therapy can help children learn new skills such as problem solving, decision making, and coping strategies. In making art, children can practice making choices, experimenting with different materials and techniques, and finding creative solutions to problems they face in the art making process.

- Third, art therapy can help children develop their social skills by providing opportunities for communication and collaboration. For example, a group art therapy session might involve working together on a collaborative art project, which can help children learn to share ideas, compromise, and work together toward a common goal.

Child art therapy is often mistaken for play therapy, but they differ in that art therapy focuses on creating a tangible product. Art therapists use their expertise of art media and artistic approaches to help children express experiences, perceptions, feelings, and imagination through creative expression. Let us examine how art therapy operates

SENSORY-BASED AND NON-VERBAL

Art therapy enables children to convey themselves through non-verbal means, allowing them to communicate in manners that may be challenging to articulate using verbal language. For example, a child who has experienced trauma may create a dark and chaotic painting that conveys their feelings of fear and confusion. Alternatively, a child who struggles with anxiety may create a soothing and repetitive pattern with colored pencils to calm their nervous system.

✓ GROWTH AND DEVELOPMENT

The creative art process, especially drawings, can offer valuable insights into a child's growth and development. Initially, a child's depiction of a person may consist of a basic circle with stick limbs, but with time, their fine motor skills and spatial awareness improve, leading to more intricate details. This awareness can be valuable in understanding a child's emotional experiences, thought processes, and sensory assimilation.

✓ SELF-REGULATION

Specific sensory features of crafting art, like the tactile sensation of sculpting clay or the rhythmic movement of brushstrokes, can prove useful in ameliorating disposition, sensory assimilation, and inducing relaxation of both body and mind. For example, a child who struggles with hyperactivity and impulsivity may benefit from the repetitive and soothing experience of finger painting.

✓ MEANING-MAKING

Art therapy offers a unique chance to use art expression as a tool to convey emotions and experiences in a symbolic manner. This approach can prove effective in exploring and processing complex emotions and experiences. For example, a child who has experienced a significant loss may create a collage that symbolizes their feelings of sadness, such as a wilted flower or a stormy sky. Through the process of creating the art piece and discussing it with the therapist, the child may begin to gain insights and make meaning out of their experience.

The bond between the child and therapist is crucial in determining the efficacy of art therapy. Art therapy is not a cure on its own, and it is important to work with a trained professional. The therapeutic process is built upon the relationship between the child and therapist. Art therapy can help repair and reshape attachment between the child and therapist through sensory and experiential means. This methodology can access initial relational states that are present prior to the dominance of language, enabling the brain to establish novel, more advantageous patterns. To perform art therapy at home, parents can encourage their children to express themselves creatively through various art mediums such as drawing, painting, or sculpting. Parents can also participate in the creative process with their children, offering support and guidance. This approach can help strengthen the parent-child bond and provide a safe space for the child to express themselves. It is important to note that while this can be a beneficial tool, it should not be a substitute for professional therapy when needed.

1.3 TOOLS AND SUPPLIES: SETTING UP A CREATIVE SPACE FOR YOUR CHILD

Let's make a creative space for your child an exciting experience! Here are some ideas and guidelines to consider:

Choose a room: Choose a place in your home where your child can create freely and undisturbed. You can consider a small table or a nook in their bedroom.

Gather supplies: To diversify their art supplies, stock up on basic materials such as paper, pencils, crayons, markers, paints, brushes, scissors, and glue. Additionally, you can get imaginative and incorporate unconventional materials such as fabrics, clay, or natural objects to add variety to their creations.

Customization: Encourage your kids to personalize their creative space by adding their own artwork or photos. You can also add an inspirational quote or positive affirmation to motivate them.

Set boundaries: Establish clear rules and boundaries with your child about what is and isn't allowed in their creative space. This may include not eating or drinking, keeping the room clean, and respecting other people's work.

Let them lead: Let your child lead the creative process and explore their own ideas and interests. Avoid giving them too much direction or criticism; instead focus on encouraging them to express themselves freely.

Encourage experimentation: Encourage your child to experiment with different art materials and techniques without worrying too much about the final product. Remember that the process of creation is as important as the end result.

Join the fun: Don't be afraid to participate in the creative process with your child. It can be a good bonding experience and a way to encourage their creativity. By following these guidelines, you can create a fun and inspiring creative space where your child can explore and express themselves through art. Remember to have fun and let your child's imagination run wild!

This checklist and providing your child with a dedicated creative space, you can foster their creativity and help them develop important skills through art-making.

ACTIVITY: SETTING UP A CREATIVE SPACE FOR YOUR CHILD

1. **Choose a space:** Decide on a dedicated area for your child's creative activities. Consider a room or a corner of a room where your child can work without interruptions.

2. **Gather supplies:** Make sure you have a variety of art supplies readily available for your child to use, including:

   ✓ Paper in various sizes and types

   ✓ Drawing materials, such as pencils, markers, crayons, and pastels

   ✓ Paints, brushes, and mixing palettes

   ✓ Glue, scissors, and tape

   ✓ Clay, play-dough, or other sculpting materials

   ✓ Collage materials, such as magazines, newspapers, and fabric scraps

3. **Organize supplies:** Keep supplies organized and within reach, so your child can find and use them easily. Consider using clear containers or shelves to store and display supplies.

4. **Create a comfortable space:** Make sure your child is comfortable while working. Provide a sturdy table and chair at an appropriate height, and add a soft rug or cushion for extra comfort.

5. **Encourage creativity:** Give your child the freedom to experiment and create without judgment. Encourage them to express themselves and their emotions through their art.

6. **Clean up:** Make sure your child knows how to clean up after their creative activities. Teach them to put away supplies and clean their workspace, so it's ready for the next time they want to create.

CHAPTER 2: COLOR THERAPY & HEALING

Color is a fascinating and ever-present aspect of our world. Children are naturally drawn to color, but how often do they think about where it comes from or how it affects their daily lives? From the vibrant colors of nature to the rainbow hues of their toys and clothes, color is an integral part of a child's world. By exploring the origins and effects of color, children can gain a deeper understanding and appreciation for the colorful world around them.

2.1. THE SCIENCE OF COLOR THERAPY: HOW DIFFERENT COLORS AFFECT OUR MOOD AND EMOTIONS

Color is everywhere in the world and it affects us in more ways than we realize. Light and energy make up color, and different wavelengths of light produce different types of colors. Visible light falls within a specific range known as the visible spectrum, which is approximately between 390 and 750 nanometers. In addition to visible light, non-visible light, such as x-rays and ultraviolet rays, possess distinct wavelengths and frequencies that can also impact us. An instance of visible light influencing us is illustrated by Seasonal Affective Disorder (SAD), which is a mild variation of depression that certain individuals undergo throughout the winter season. This happens because during the winter, we get less exposure to natural light and our bodies produce less vitamin D. This can make us feel tired, moody, and even depressed.

Art therapy can be a helpful tool in combating SAD and other forms of depression. By using different colors and exploring how they make us feel, we can tap into the emotional and psychological effects of color. For example, warm colors like red, orange, and yellow can make us feel energized and happy, while cool colors like blue and green can have a calming and soothing effect. By incorporating different colors into art therapy sessions, we can help children and adults express their emotions and feelings in a safe and supportive environment.

AN OVERVIEW OF CHROMO-THERAPY

Chromo-therapy, also called color therapy or light therapy, is a holistic method of healing that involves the utilization of the visible light spectrum to improve a person's physical and mental well-being. The distinctive vibrational frequency of each color is thought to provide specific properties that can impact the energy and frequencies within our bodies.

Light can infiltrate our bodies through both the skin and eyes, with some people believing that particular colors can trigger hormones and elicit chemical reactions that affect emotions and promote healing. Color therapy is a variation of art therapy, which utilizes colors to help children express themselves and regulate their emotions. Each color has a distinct impact on a person's mood and emotional state. For instance, blue has a calming effect and can lead to lower blood pressure, while green can help emotionally unbalanced children to relax. Yellow may also be used to stimulate children who are experiencing depression.

These therapies suggest that a person's aura contains various light layers that can be used for purification and balance. Understanding the colors present in a child's aura can assist parents in comprehending their child's spirit and how to facilitate healing. The colors surrounding children can also have different impacts, and they can be employed in art therapy sessions to promote emotional regulation and healing

2.2. COLORING FOR CALMNESS: MINDFUL COLORING ACTIVITIES TO SOOTHE ANXIETY AND STRESS

Coloring for calmness is a form of art therapy that can help children soothe anxiety and stress. This activity involves using coloring books and pencils to create beautiful and calming designs, patterns and images.

When children engage in coloring, it allows them to focus their attention on a specific task, which can help them feel more centered and relaxed. It also encourages the use of fine motor skills, which can help children regulate their breathing and heart rate, reducing stress and anxiety.

For example, imagine your child is feeling anxious about an upcoming test at school. You can help them ease their anxiety by sitting down with them and coloring together. You can choose a coloring book that has calming designs, such as mandalas, or scribbling.

As you color together, encourage your child to focus on the colors, the patterns, and the movement of their hand as they fill in the spaces. This can help them redirect their attention away from their anxious thoughts and into the present moment.

Coloring for calmness can also be used as a regular self-care practice for children, helping them develop coping skills for managing stress and anxiety. Encourage your child to color for a few minutes every day, and help them create a special space in your home where they can relax and engage in this activity.

Calm coloring is a process that children can engage in to help reduce anxiety and stress levels. Here are some steps kids can take:

1. Choose a coloring book or page that you find attractive.

2. Choose a color you like to use.

3. Find a quiet and comfortable place to paint.

4. Breathe slowly and deeply as you paint, concentrating on each stroke of the paint tool.

5. Participate in the painting process and let go of any distracting thoughts or worries.

6. Take breaks when needed and return to painting when you feel more relaxed.

This process helps children focus on the present, bringing a sense of peace and relaxation to their minds and bodies. It is also a fun and creative way for children to express themselves and their feelings.

ACTIVITY: MINDFULNESS COLORING WORKSHEET

Instructions:

1. Choose a quiet and comfortable place to sit.

2. Color the following page with desired colors.

3. Take a deep breath and let it out slowly. Repeat this several times to calm your mind.

4. Start coloring the paper, pay attention to the lines and shapes to be colored.

5. Take your time painting and enjoy the process.

6. If your mind starts to wander, pay close attention to the coloring.

7. After you finish coloring your paper, take some time to observe your work and notice the colors and patterns you are using.

8. Take another deep breath, then exhale slowly.

Questions:

1. How did you feel before you started painting?

_____

_____

2. Does coloring make you feel calmer? If so, how?

_____

_____

3. What color do you use most often when painting?

_____

_____

4. Did you notice any patterns or designs as you painted?

_____

_____

5. How did you feel when you finished painting?

_____

_____

Coloring is a simple and effective way to calm the mind and reduce anxiety and stress. Use this worksheet to practice mindful coloring and experience the benefits for yourself.

2.3. RAINBOW MEDITATION: USING COLORS TO EXPLORE AND EXPRESS EMOTIONS

Rainbows have been having a significant meaning throughout history and have symbolized hope, faith, and better times to come, especially after a storm. They can help children learn to connect with their inner selves, energy, and emotions through practicing yoga and mindfulness. Rainbows are formed from light energy, which is made up of seven different colors, also known as the visible light spectrum. Traditional practices associate these colors with various energy centers or chakras in the body, each corresponding to a particular location and color of the visible light spectrum, starting from the base of the spine to the top of the head. Exploring these energy centers and colors can help children develop self-awareness and create a language around their emotions. Each energy center and color is also linked to different qualities that children can cultivate in their lives, promoting confidence, empathy, and emotional regulation. Encouraging children to notice their own inner state and being present with the energy of their peers and the group can also be helpful.

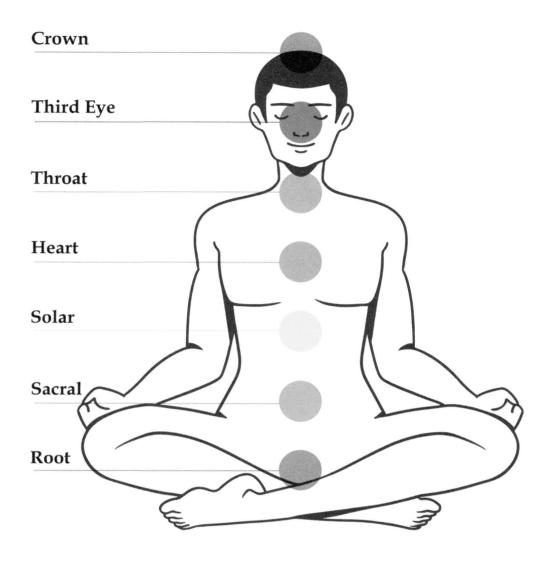

Crown

Third Eye

Throat

Heart

Solar

Sacral

Root

This yoga lesson plan is a fun and interactive way for kids to explore energy, rainbows and colors. The lesson plan includes different yoga poses and movements that correspond to the colors of the rainbow and their associated energy centers in the body. The sequence starts with a warm up that honors the sun and incorporates common yoga poses such as Downward Dog and Plank Pose. Next, there are fun activities such as the Umbrella Up and Be A Rain Cloud poses that build strength and self-awareness. Finally, children are encouraged to make rainbows with their bodies using various yoga poses like Warrior Pose and Downward Dog.

By practicing this yoga sequence, children can learn about the connection between light, energy, and rainbows. They can also explore their own energy centers through yoga and mindfulness. The Rainbow Chakra Relaxation at the end of the sequence is a great way to help children unwind and connect with their inner selves. Overall, this yoga sequence can promote self-awareness, confidence, empathy, and emotional regulation in children.

As parents, we all want to help our children develop in the best possible way. That's why I want to share with you a list of powerful and effective rainbow activities that can support your child's development. These activities include sensory play, crafts, fine motor and visual motor exercises, as well as movement ideas. By engaging in these fun and creative activities, your child can enhance their motor skills, cognitive abilities, and emotional well-being. So, let's explore the magic of rainbows together!

Rainbow Coloring: Let your kids color the given rainbow with all the rainbow colors. You can also ask them draw their own rainbow and color it.

Rainbow Mandala: Give the children a blank mandala and colored pencils, markers, or paint. Ask them to color each part of the mandala with a different color of the rainbow.

Rainbow Salt Dough: Serve kids with salt dough in different colors. Have them create a rainbow or other rainbow-inspired creations.

Rainbow Sensory Bottle: Give kids a clear bottle and colorful objects like beads, glitter, and tinsel. Have them fill the bottles with different colors for a rainbow effect.

Rainbow sand craft: Give kids different colored sand and a clear bottle or jar. Ask them to apply colors to the sand to create a rainbow effect.

Rainbow Beads: Give them colorful beads and strings. Have them make a rainbow bracelet or necklace.

Rainbow Stained Glass: Provide them tissue paper and transparent contact paper for in different colors of the rainbow. Have them make a rainbow of colored glass by gluing tissue paper to contact paper.

2.4. CREATING A PERSONAL COLOR WHEEL: UNDERSTANDING YOUR CHILD'S EMOTIONAL PALETTE

Creating a personal color wheel can be a valuable art therapy exercise for children, helping them understand and express their emotional palette. By recognizing colors and associating them with different emotions, children can learn to communicate and regulate their emotions more effectively. This activity can also help parents gain insight into the child's emotional state and provide support and guidance accordingly. It gives children a safe and creative outlet to  process and express their feelings, improving emotional intelligence, self-confidence and self-esteem. Additionally, creating a personal color wheel can be a fun and engaging activity that encourages creativity and self-expression. Kids can use the template od color wheel given below. This can be done using a variety of art materials such as paints, markers or colored pencils and can be tailored to your child's individual needs and preferences.

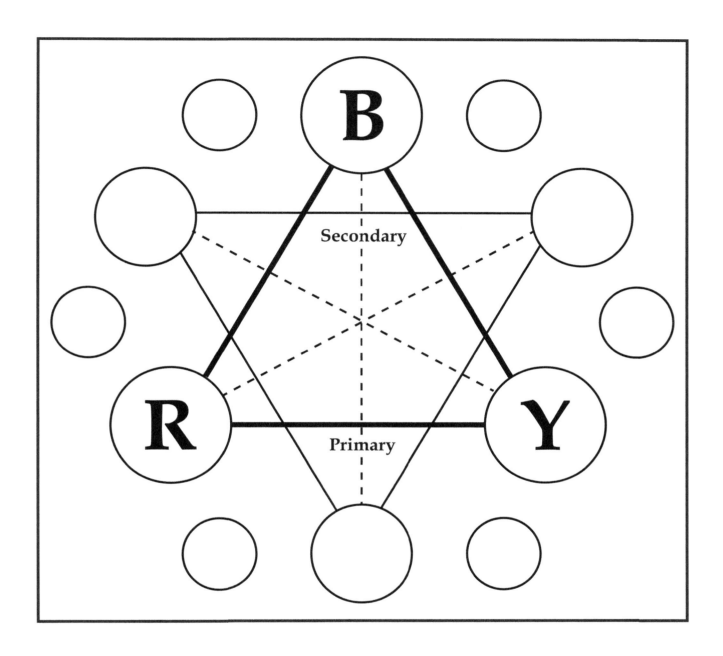

Sentiments Color Wheel

The Color Wheel of Sentiments is a simple yet effective activity for children and teenagers to explore their emotions in a creative way. It also presents an opportunity for parents to engage in discussions with their children about their emotions. Even if you're not an artist, you can still participate in this activity with your child.

You can help your child create a Color Wheel of Sentiments by providing them with a blank piece of white paper or poster board and some colored pencils, markers, or crayons.

Ask them to draw a circle and divide it into eight slices by making a + and x on the circle. Let your child choose the eight emotions they want to include on their Color Wheel, but you can suggest some ideas to help them. After that, ask them to write the name of each emotion on each slice outside the circle. They can then fill in each slice with a color or draw a representation of each emotion. Discuss their choices with them and ask them to explain why they chose each emotion and how they represented it in the circle.

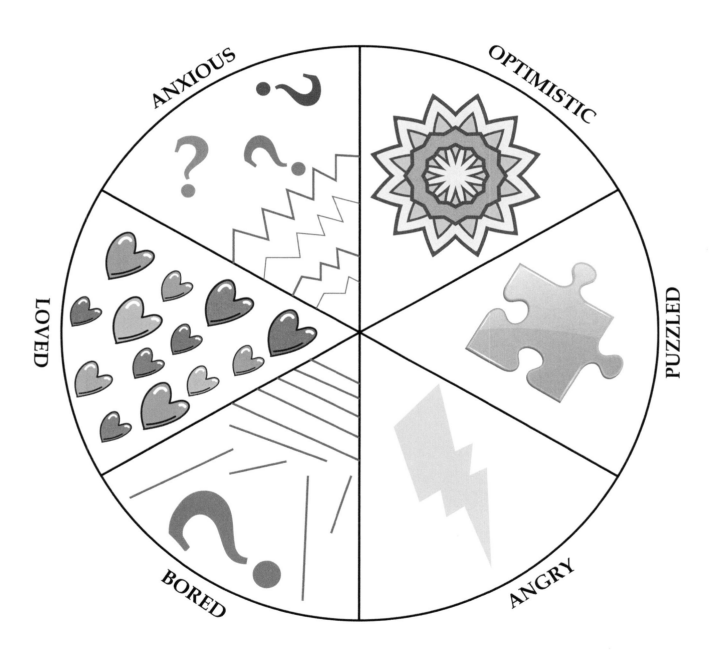

Now it's your turn:

MY SENTIMENTS WHEEL

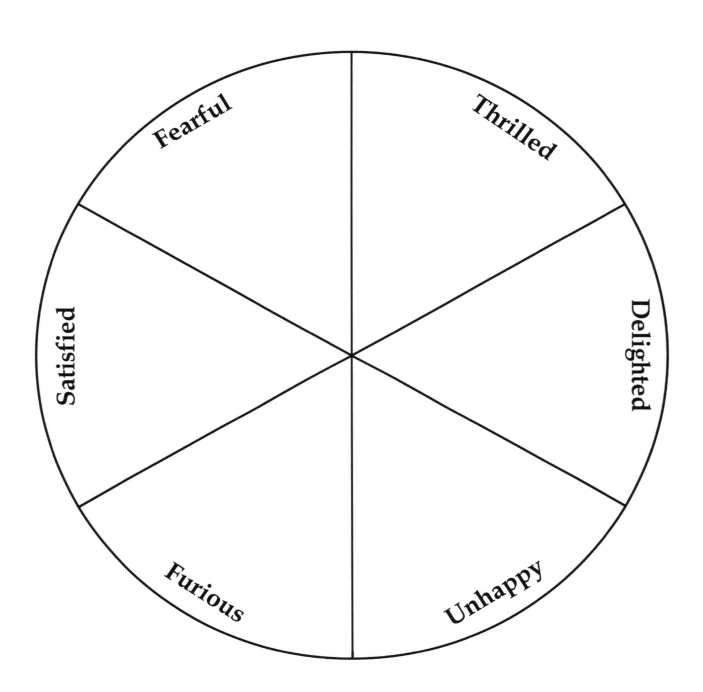

2.5. COLOR THE EMOTION

Color the Emotion art therapy is a creative and effective way for kids to express and manage their emotions. This therapy involves using colors and art to represent different emotions, allowing children to explore their feelings in a safe and enjoyable way. This therapy can also help children communicate their emotions more effectively and develop emotional intelligence.

To begin the therapy, children are provided with a blank sheet of paper and a range of colored pencils, crayons or markers. They are then asked to choose a color that represents how they are feeling, and to use that color to fill in the entire sheet of paper. For example, if a child is feeling sad, they might choose blue to represent their emotions.

After they have filled in the sheet with the chosen color, children are asked to add other colors to the picture to represent any other emotions they might be feeling. For example, if they are feeling angry, they might add some red to their picture.

Once the child has finished coloring, they can then be asked to talk about their picture and their emotions. Parents can ask open-ended questions to encourage their child to share their thoughts and feelings, such as "What made you choose that color?" or "What does this picture represent to you?"

This therapy can be done regularly as a way for children to check in with their emotions and express themselves. It is also a great way for parents to connect with their child and help them manage their emotions in a healthy way.

Color the emotions represented as scoops of ice cream.

Children can have a great time exploring the wonderful world of color by using mouse paint art. They get to dip their cotton ball mice into the different colors and mix them together to create new shades and hues. This activity is not only a fun way to play with color but can also be a form of art therapy, allowing children to express themselves and explore their emotions through color.

LET'S GROOVE IN SOME HUES

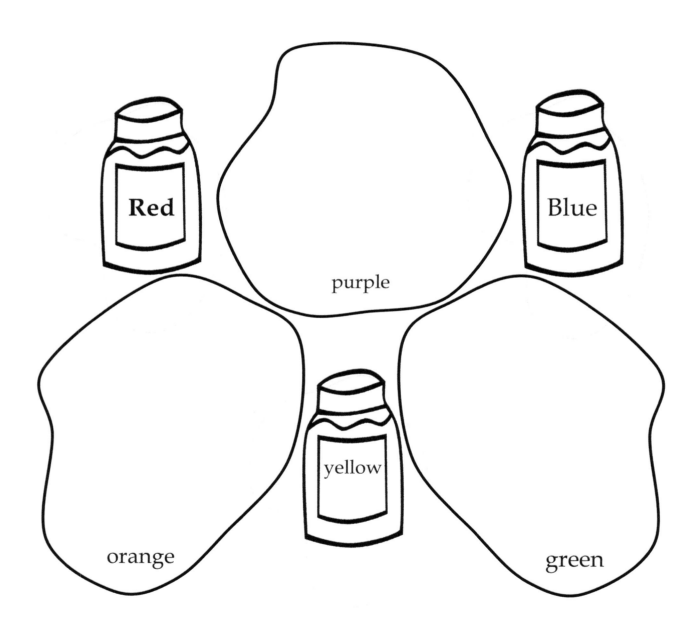

DRAW THE FACE THAT FOLLOWS

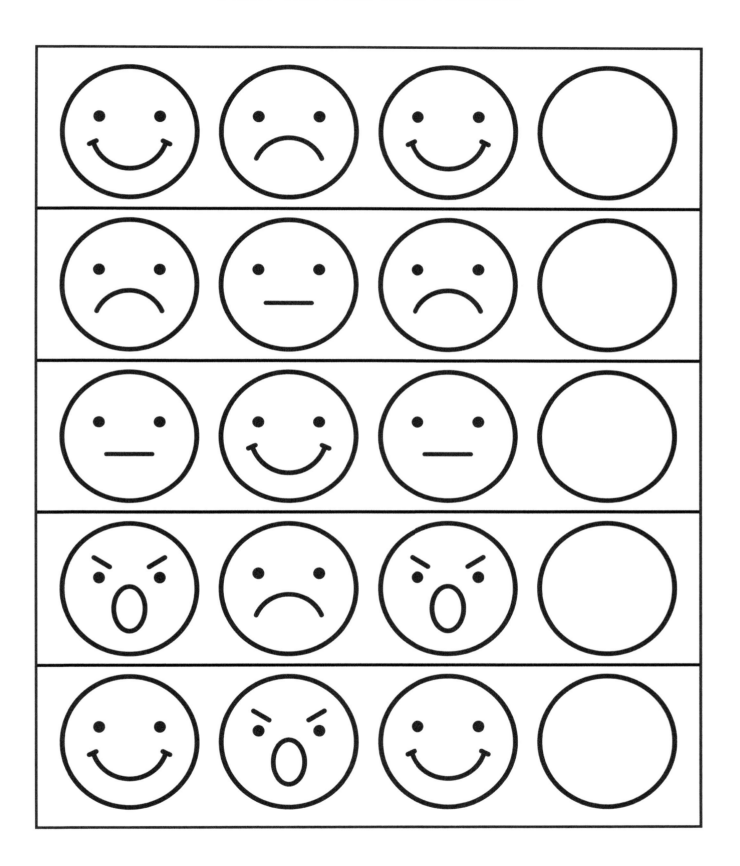

Emotion Cards are a tool used to help individuals identify and communicate their emotions through a set of facial expressions.

EMOTION CARDS

Joyful

Distressed

Astonished

Furious

WHAT HAPPENED THIS WEEK?

Color in all the things that you did this past week, then talk about it!: Mark the activities you engaged in during the week, then discuss them.

Outburst of Anger

Became harsh

Shed tears

Broke a rule or school policy

Contentment

Physically assaulted

Cinema

Employed a strategy to manage stress

Apprehension

Humiliated

High score

Acquainted myself with a new person

Was praised

Frustration

Took something without permission

Hosted a friend

Experienced intimidation

Made something new

Completed assignment

Engaged in a recreational activity

Remained at home due to an illness

Provided false information

Engaged in a verbal or physical argument

CHAPTER 3: SELF-EXPLORATION AND HEALING THROUGH MANDALA ART

Have you heard of mandala art therapy? It's a form of art therapy that has been used for centuries and is known for its spiritual significance and representation of wholeness. The process of creating a mandala is not only therapeutic but also symbolic, as the shapes and colors you choose reflect your inner self at the time of creation.

For children, creating a mandala can be a wonderful way to express their emotions and feelings in a creative way. By allowing their instincts and feelings to guide them through the process of creation, they can create a portrait of themselves that represents how they are feeling at that particular moment.

The beauty of mandala art therapy is that it's not about the final product, but rather the journey. As they create their mandala, children can explore their emotions and gain a deeper understanding of themselves. And when they are finished, they will have a unique and personal representation of themselves that they can be proud of.

3.1. MANDALA ART THERAPY: A CREATIVE JOURNEY TOWARDS SELF-DISCOVERY AND HEALING

Have you heard of mandala art activities for kids? It's a fun and therapeutic way for children to express themselves and explore their emotions through art. While the circle serves as the core of mandala designs, there are no restrictions or guidelines regarding the colors or materials that can be used. Children have the freedom to choose from a range of art supplies, including colored pencils, pastels, markers, oils, watercolors, and others. They can choose to draw or paint on any surface of their liking, whether it is paper, canvas, or poster board. To get started, find a quiet space for your child to work on their mandala. This will help them to focus and connect with their inner selves. Encourage your child to let their feelings and emotions inspire them as they create their mandala art. There is no right or wrong way to do this, so they can let their creativity flow freely.

Upon completing their mandala, encourage your child to reflect on their color choices, taking note of any colors that were frequently used or underutilized. They should also analyze the shapes and patterns in their creation, paying attention to the lines, edges, and contrasts within the image. Finally, prompt them to write down their emotions and memories that the mandala evokes, delving into the details.

The process of creating a mandala can be very personal and introspective, so the results will vary from child to child. But the goal is for your child to gain a deeper understanding of themselves through the art of mandala. By reflecting on their creation and the emotions and memories it evokes, your child can experience self-healing, self-expression, and self-exploration.

The use of mandala art therapy is known to aid in the enhancement of children and adolescents' coping mechanisms and emotional regulation. Participating in the creative process can provide a sense of authority and proficiency over their emotions, leading to a decrease in anxiety and stress levels.

The phrase "Sentiment Wheel" refers to a visual tool that categorizes and organizes emotions into different groups or categories, usually in the form of a circle or wheel. Each section of the wheel represents a different emotion or feeling, and the wheel can be used to help people identify and articulate their emotions.

SENTIMENT WHEEL

Displeased	Perplexed	Exhausted	Furious
Ashamed	Aloof	Terrible	Unhappy
Serene	Uncertain	Welcomed	Defenseless
Surprised	Strong	Uninterested	Resentful
Hostile	Astonished	Miserable	Let down
Occupied	Furious	Irritated	Joyful
Revolted	Satisfied	Isolated	Hopeful
Injured	Enthusiastic	Revolted	Frightened
Mischievous	Curious	Reliable	Frail
Anxious	Afraid	Negative	Pleased
Astonished	Disappointed	Hopeless	Intimidated
Confused	Excluded	Remorseful	Worried
			Judgmental

Various Techniques of Mandala

There are many mandala techniques and shapes that children can follow. Here are some:

- ✓ **Freeform Mandala:** This is a great technique for younger children who may not be ready for more complex mandala designs. Give them a blank circle and some drawing supplies (like markers, crayons, or crayons) and let them draw and color whatever they want.

✓ **Symmetrical Mandalas:** Symmetrical mandalas are a great way to teach children about balance and symmetry. You can start by drawing a straight line through the center of the circle and then ask your child to draw the same design on each side of the line.

✓ **Geometric Mandalas:** Geometric mandalas use repeating geometric shapes (such as triangles, squares, and circles) to create intricate designs. This can be a fun and challenging activity for older children who enjoy puzzles and problem solving.

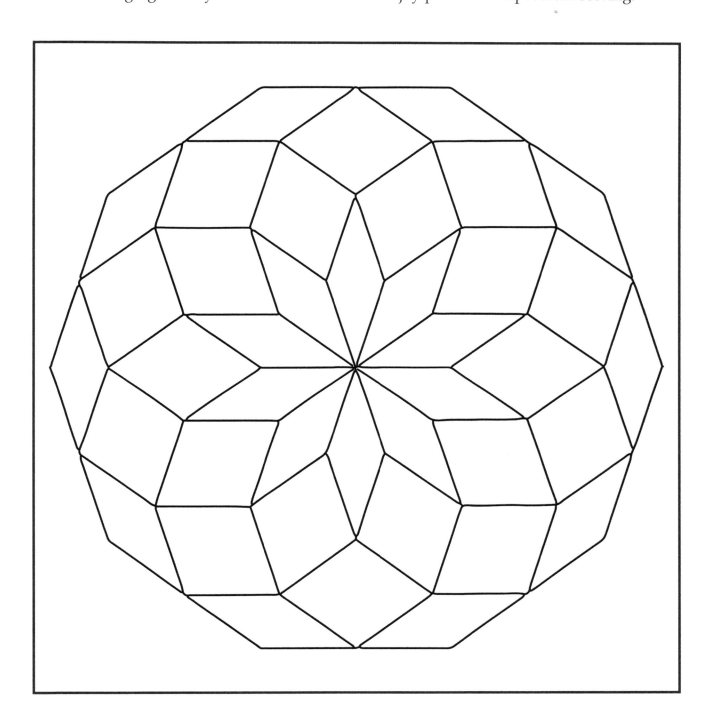

✓ **Nature Mandalas:** Nature mandalas are a great way to incorporate natural materials (like leaves, flowers, and rocks) into your mandala design. Gather some materials from your garden or a nearby park and arrange them in a circular pattern.

✓ **Mandala Coloring Pages:** One great way to introduce your child to the world of mandala art is by providing them with mandala coloring pages. These pages can easily be created by drawing a mandala design on a piece of paper and making copies of it. Then, your child can use their favorite art supplies to color in the pre-drawn design. Not only is this a fun and easy way for kids to get started with mandala art, but it also helps them to develop their coloring skills and fine motor abilities. As they progress, they can begin to create their own mandala designs using the techniques and forms they have learned from coloring pages.

Whatever mandala technique or shape your child chooses, the most important thing is that they can explore their creativity and express themselves in a way that feels comfortable and natural to them.

3.2. CREATING A PERSONAL MANDALA: EXPLORING YOUR CHILD'S INNER WORLD AND EMOTIONS

On a surface like canvas or paper, various drawing materials such as colored pencils, pastels, markers, and watercolors would be used to create a personal mandala. The center of the mandala design is a circle that can be formed using a compass or any other circular object. This circular shape will form the foundation for the remainder of the drawing.

Once the circle is drawn, kids can start adding different forms, lines, and colors to their mandala. There are no rules or restrictions when it comes to mandala art, and children are encouraged to let their instincts and emotions guide them. This creative process can be a form of self-expression and provides opportunities for children to express their feelings, thoughts and experiences non-verbally.

After completing their mandala, children can reflect on the colors, shapes, and designs they used. They can take note of any predominant or least-used colors and analyze the shapes and designs they created. This reflection can help children gain a deeper understanding of their inner self and emotions, and can also provide an opportunity for self-exploration and self-healing.

Mandala art can be an effective tool to help children manage their behavior in a positive way. By creating their own mandalas, children can learn to express their emotions and feelings creatively and non-verbally. This can help them develop a greater sense of self-awareness and improve their ability to communicate their emotions to others.

The process of creating a mandala can also promote mindfulness and concentration, as children are encouraged to be present in the moment and fully participate in the creative process. This can help them develop better attention and concentration skills, which can translate into improved behavior and academic performance. Additionally, mandala art can be a fun and entertaining activity for children that can help reduce stress and promote feelings of relaxation and calm. By providing children with a safe and creative outlet for their emotions, they are less likely to engage in negative behavior.

3.3. GROUP MANDALA: BUILDING COMMUNICATION AND SOCIAL SKILLS THROUGH ART

Group mandala is an interactive and collaborative art activity that allows children to express their creativity while building communication and social skills. The activity involves having a group of children work together to create a single mandala design. Each child contributes their own unique element to the design, resulting in a beautiful and cohesive final product.

To get started with group mandala, gather a group of children and provide them with a large piece of paper or canvas to work on. Then, have them sit in a circle around the paper and take turns adding to the design. Each child can add their own unique element to the mandala, such as a specific color or pattern, and then pass the paper to the next person in the circle.

As the mandala design grows, encourage the children to communicate with one another about what they are adding and how it fits into the overall design. This helps to build social and communication skills, as the children learn to listen to and collaborate with one another. It also fosters a sense of community and teamwork, as each child's contribution is valued and important to the final product.

3.4. CREATING A VISION BOARD

Creating a vision board is a powerful form of art therapy that can help children manifest their goals, dreams and desires. It involves using pictures, words and phrases to create a visual representation of what they want to achieve or manifest in their life. The process of creating a vision board is meant to be a fun and creative experience that engages the child's imagination and intuition.

To make a visual chalkboard, you'll need construction paper or another type of durable paper or cardstock, along with a variety of magazines, newspapers, and drawing supplies such as scissors, glue, markers, and stickers. The child can then cut out pictures, words and phrases that resonate with them and arrange them on the board in a meaningful and inspiring way. As your child works on their vision board, they will explore their hopes, dreams and aspirations and be able to express their emotions and feelings creatively and constructively. They can also discover new insights and perspectives on what they want to achieve in life.

Once the vision board is ready, the child can hang it in their room or in another exposed place where he can see it every day. This serves as a constant reminder of their goals and can motivate them to take action to achieve them.

Here are some techniques for creating a vision board that parents can use to guide their children:

Cut and Paste: This is the most basic technique in which the child cuts out pictures and words from magazines or newspapers and glues them onto a board.

Draw and Paint: Kids can also draw or paint their vision board. They can use different colors and materials to create a visual representation of their dreams and aspirations.

Collage: A collage is a technique in which the child combines different materials such as fabrics, buttons and ribbons to create a textured and layered bulletin board.

Mind Mapping: This technique involves writing words or sentences that describe the child's goals and dreams and drawing lines to connect them.

Remember that the most important thing for the child is to express themselves creatively and have fun with the process.

VISUALIZATION BOARD

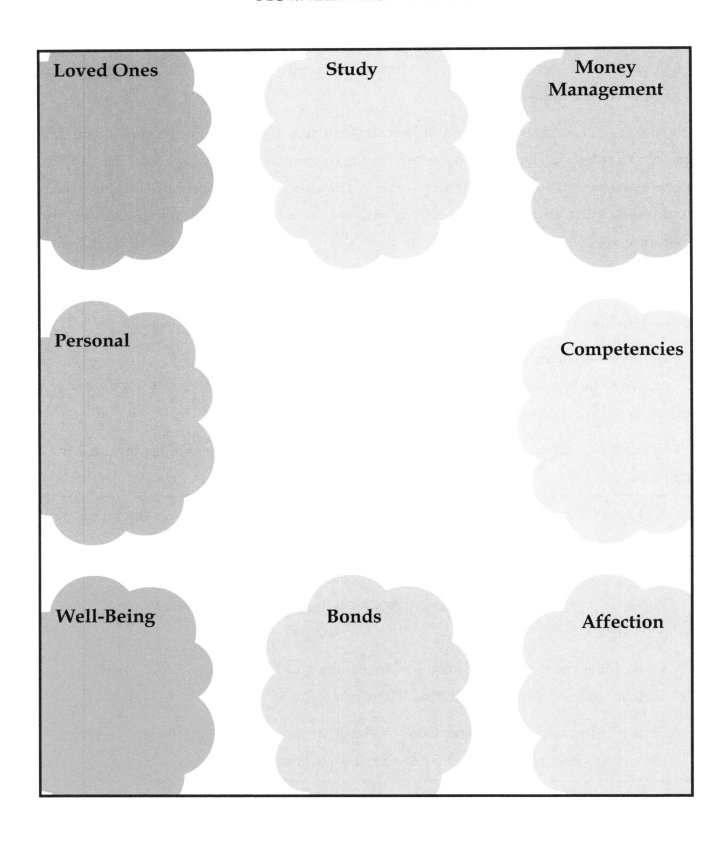

Loved Ones

Study

Money Management

Personal

Competencies

Well-Being

Bonds

Affection

CHAPTER 4: TRANSFORMATIONAL SELF PORTRAIT ART THERAPY ACTIVITY

Children also go through changes and transformations as they grow up. Some changes might be small, while others can be big and noticeable. These transformations help shape their personalities and who they become as they grow older. Sometimes, children might not even realize they have changed until after the fact. But what about when children want to make a deliberate change within themselves? Transformational art therapy can be beneficial for them. It can help children explore their past transformations/changes and also help them envision and work towards their future transformations/changes.

4.1. THE ART OF SELF-PORTRAITURE: UNDERSTANDING AND EXPRESSING PERSONAL IDENTITY AND EMOTIONS

Transformational art therapy is a way for children to express themselves creatively while also exploring their inner thoughts and emotions. It can help children cope with difficult experiences, whether it's dealing with the loss of a loved one, adjusting to a new school, or just struggling with their emotions. Through art therapy, children can gain insight into their feelings and behaviors and learn new ways to cope with challenging situations.

For example, if a child has experienced a traumatic event, such as a car accident or the loss of a pet, they may feel overwhelmed with emotions that are difficult to express through words alone. Art therapy can provide a safe space for the child to express their feelings and work through the trauma at their own pace. Through their art, they can begin to process their emotions and find ways to heal.

On the other hand, if a child is struggling with their self-esteem or confidence, art therapy can be used as a tool to help build a more positive self-image. By creating art that focuses on their strengths and accomplishments, they can develop a more positive outlook on themselves and their abilities.

The activity is rooted in the principles of transformational therapy and art therapy, which can assist in navigating significant life changes. Throughout life, individuals undergo various transformations, and it is crucial to reflect on our experiences and the ways they impact us. This particular activity aims to facilitate reflection on a negative past experience, its present effects, and to identify potential areas for self-improvement.

To begin this art therapy exercise, prompt your child to identify a past experience that is still affecting them negatively in some way. It can be a recent event or something that happened long ago. Encourage them to reflect on the details of the experience and how it continues to impact their life today. You may suggest that they write down their thoughts to help organize their ideas.

Once they have reflected on their past experiences, encourage your child to think about how they would like to transform themselves as a result. This may involve changes related to their self-confidence, self-confidence, conceptual or emotional state, or other areas of personal growth.

With this reflection in mind, your child can now begin creating a transforming self-portrait mural using any medium of their choice, such as painting, drawing, or collage. Encourage them to explore their creativity and experiment with various materials.

As they create their self-portrait, prompt your child to consider how they want to represent themselves. Do they wish to portray their transformation from a negative experience to a positive one? Would they like to showcase their strength and confidence? Or would they prefer to symbolically represent their emotions? There are no right or wrong answers, so encourage your child to express themselves authentically.

After completing the self-portrait, ask your child to explain their work to you, describing the colors, shapes, and symbols they used and their meaning. Encourage them to share their thoughts and feelings about the artwork and how it relates to their past experiences and their desired transformation.

This art therapy exercise is designed to assist children in reflecting on their life experiences and how they have influenced their sense of self. It is a three-part activity involving the creation of a transformational self-portrait mural.

This self-portrait activity is divided into three parts. For the first part, your child will reflect on a negative experience from their past that impacted their sense of self and create a self-portrait based on that experience. The second part involves creating a self-portrait that reflects how they feel about themselves today, as a result of that experience. Finally, the third part is focused on creating an image of their ideal future self, after they have transformed from the negative experience. Encourage your child to be creative and expressive in each part of the self-portrait.

PUTTING IT ALL TOGETHER:

Once your child has completed all three pieces of the self-portrait, encourage them to reflect on their artwork and identify elements that reflect their transformation from the negative experience and the transformation they desire. The ideal future self-portrait can serve as a reminder and inspiration to work towards becoming the image they have created.

4.2. THE POWER OF SYMBOLS: CREATING PERSONAL SYMBOLISM AND METAPHORS IN ART

"The Power of Symbols: Creating Personal Symbolism and Metaphor in Art" is an art therapy activity that encourages children to express themselves through symbols and metaphors. It is a great way for children to explore their inner world and gain insight into their feelings, thoughts and experiences.

Start it by saying that symbols are powerful tools that can help children express complex emotions and experiences in creative and meaningful ways. In this activity, children are asked to create their own symbols and metaphors that represent different aspects of their lives, such as their dreams, fears, hopes and relationships.

For starters, parents can encourage their children to brainstorm different symbols and metaphors that appeal to them. For example, a child may use a tree to symbolize growth and change, or a bird to symbolize freedom and independence. Parents can help their children by asking open-ended questions and offering support and advice.

Once the child has chosen their symbols, they can begin to create a work of art that incorporates those symbols and metaphors. It can be done with any medium like drawing, painting, collage or sculpture. As the child works on their art, parents can encourage them to think about their symbols and what they represent. The end product will be a one-of-a-kind work of art filled with personal meaning and symbolism. By creating these symbols and metaphors, children can better understand themselves and their experiences, and develop new ways of expressing themselves in creative and meaningful ways.

TITLE: MY PERSONAL SYMBOLS

Introduction:

Symbols are objects or images that represent something else. They can be found in everyday life, in nature, and in art. They have different meanings and can evoke different emotions. In this worksheet, you will create your own personal symbols that represent important things in your life.

Instructions:

Think about things that are important to you, such as your family, friends, hobbies, or beliefs.

Write down a list of words that describe these things.

_____

_____

_____

_____

_____

_____

_____

_____

Next to each word, draw a simple symbol or image that represents that word.

You can use any medium to create your symbols, such as pencils, markers, or paint.

Once you have created your symbols, think about how you can use them in your art. You can create a painting or collage that incorporates your symbols, or you can create a story or poem that uses your symbols as metaphors.

Example:

Word: Family

Symbol: A heart with the word "family" written inside

Word: Friendship

Symbol: Two hands holding each other

Word: Nature

Symbol: A tree with roots and leaves

Word: Adventure

Symbol: A compass pointing north

Conclusion:

Symbols can be powerful tools in art and in life. They can help us express our emotions, communicate our ideas, and connect with others. By creating your own personal symbols, you can add more meaning and depth to your art and create something truly unique.

Coloring sheets featuring the peace symbol can be a helpful tool in art therapy for children, allowing them to express themselves creatively while promoting a sense of calm and relaxation.

4.3. FROM INSIDE OUT: EXPLORING AND EXPRESSING INNER FEELINGS THROUGH SELF-PORTRAITS

From the Inside Out: Exploring and Expressing Inner Feelings Through Self-Portrait is an activity that encourages children to explore and express their emotions through self-portraits.

In this activity, children are guided to think about their own emotions, such as happiness, sadness, anger or fear, and how they manifest in their body and face. They are encouraged to use color, line and shape to depict these emotions in their self-portraits. Through this process, children can gain a deeper understanding of their emotions and learn to express them in healthy and creative ways.

To get started, kids can gather materials like paper, pencils, crayons, and markers. Your kid can then follow these steps:

1. Think of a specific emotion that you would like to explore and express through your self-portrait.

2. Close your eyes and focus on how that emotion feels in your body. Where do you feel it? What does it do?

3. Open your eyes and draw a self-portrait using colors, lines and shapes to represent this emotion.

Encourage them to use bold colors for strong emotions and softer colors for subtler emotions.

After completing the self-portrait, ask them to think about what they have created. What emotions are represented in the artwork? How do colors, lines and shapes help convey those emotions?

Finally, encourage them to share their artwork with an adult or trusted friend and discuss their emotions and what they have learned from this activity.

Create a visual representation of yourself by drawing and coloring the outer portion of a face, and then depict your hobbies, emotions, thoughts, and feelings on the inside. Take inspiration from the sample photo provided for guidance.

ME

The Visible Self worksheet helps kids identify and express the parts of themselves that are easily seen by others, such as their interests and personality traits.

The Hidden Self worksheet encourages kids to explore and express the parts of themselves that may not be as visible to others, such as their emotions, fears, and insecurities.

Now it's your turn to draw your visible and hidden self

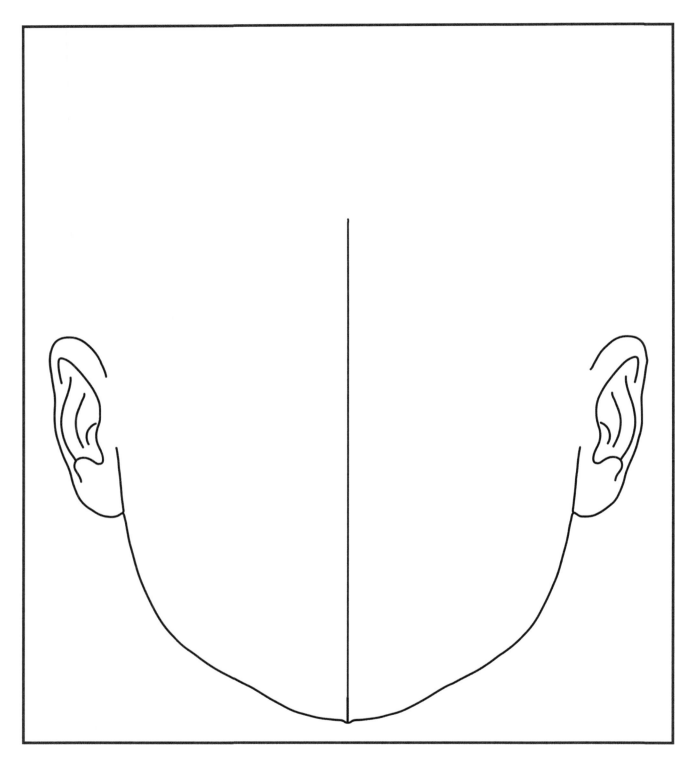

Visible Self   Hidden Self

4.4. GROUP SELF-PORTRAIT: ENHANCING SOCIAL SKILLS AND EMPATHY THROUGH ART

Group Self-Portrait is an art activity that involves creating a self-portrait as a group. This activity helps children develop their social skills and empathy towards others by working collaboratively to create a final piece of art.

To begin, children can gather in a group and decide on a theme for their self-portrait. It could be based on a shared experience or interest, such as a class trip or a favorite hobby. Once they have decided on a theme, they can start creating their individual self-portraits using art materials like paint, markers, and colored pencils.

As the children are working on their self-portraits, they can talk about their choices and share their thoughts and feelings with each other. This is a great opportunity for children to practice their social skills and develop empathy towards others. They can learn to listen to others and appreciate different perspectives, and they can also offer support and encouragement to their peers.

Once the individual self-portraits are complete, the children can work together to create a final group self-portrait. They can decide on a composition and arrange their individual self-portraits in a way that reflects their theme. This part of the activity encourages teamwork and collaboration, as the children work together to create a cohesive final product.

When the group self-portrait is complete, the children can reflect on their experience and share their thoughts and feelings about the activity. This is another opportunity for children to practice their social skills and empathy towards others, as they learn to communicate their thoughts and feelings in a respectful and supportive way.

4.5. CREATIVE WRITING AND JOURNALING

Creative writing and journaling are forms of art therapy that involve using writing as a way to express emotions, thoughts, and experiences. It can be a helpful tool for children to process their feelings and experiences in a safe and creative way.

To get started with creative writing and journaling, all you need is a pen or pencil and a notebook or piece of paper. Encourage your child to write down anything that comes to mind, without worrying about grammar or spelling. They can write about their day, their dreams, their hopes and fears, or anything else that is on their mind.

Writing can be a powerful way to explore emotions and express oneself. It can help children to identify and understand their feelings, and to communicate them in a way that feels safe and non-judgmental. In addition, creative writing and journaling can improve literacy skills and encourage a love of writing.

Encourage your child to set aside time each day or week for creative writing and journaling. You can provide prompts or writing exercises to help get them started, or they can simply write about whatever is on their mind. Remember to create a safe and supportive environment for your child to share their writing if they choose to do so.

Here are some ideas of creative writing and journaling

Free Writing: Encourage your child to write freely without worrying about spelling, grammar or punctuation. The idea is to let the words flow across the paper. This can be a great way for your child to express themselves and their feelings.

Character Creation: Have your child create a character, real or fictional, and write about their experiences. This can be a way for them to explore different emotions and situations in a safe and creative way.

Stream of Consciousness Writing: Similar to free writing, this technique involves writing whatever comes into your mind without thinking about it. It can be a great way for your child to put their thoughts and feelings on paper.

Write poetry: Encourage your child to write poetry to explore their emotions and feelings. Poetry can be a great way to creatively express complex emotions.

Gratitude Journal: Encourage your child to write down things they're grateful for every day. This can help them focus on the positives in their lives and cultivate a sense of gratitude and appreciation.

I FEEL GRATEFUL FOR

Dream Journal: encouraging your child to keep a dream journal is a wonderful way to help them explore their inner world, gain insight into their emotions and thoughts, and nurture their creativity and imagination. It's a simple yet powerful practice that can have a positive impact on their mental and emotional well-being.

Collage Journal: Instead of writing, encourage your child to make a collage of pictures that represent their emotions or feelings. It can be a great way for them to express themselves visually.

Make Lists: Encourage your child to make lists of their favorite things, things they're good at, things they want to accomplish, etc. It can be a way for them to focus on their strengths and goals.

"I AM AN INDIVIDUAL WHO"

"Fill in the following sentences to express more about yourself:"

I am a one who adores _____

I am a one who loathes _____

I am a one who is unable to _____

I am a one who has the ability to _____

I am a one who refuses to _____

I am a one who possesses _____

I am a one who is excited to _____

I am a one who would choose to _____

I am a one who has yet to _____

I am a one who desires to _____

I am a one who attempted to _____

I am a one who is frequently ignored _____

I am a one who appreciates _____

I am a one who never misses to _____

I am a one who frequently overlooks to _____

I am a one who is unfamiliar with how to _____

I am a one who craves _____

I am a one who is popular _____

Keep a Mindfulness Journal: Encourage your child to write about their mindfulness experiences. This can be a way for them to explore their emotions and feelings in the present moment.

Write letters: Encourage your child to write letters to themselves or others and express their feelings and emotions. This can be a way to work through your emotions and communicate with others in a confident and creative way.

A LETTER TO ME

CHAPTER 5: GARDEN PHOTOGRAPHY

Garden photography is a unique form of art therapy for kids that combines the beauty of nature with the power of the camera lens. It allows children to express themselves creatively while also fostering a deeper connection with the natural world. Through garden photography, kids can explore their surroundings, develop their creativity, and cultivate mindfulness by slowing down and truly observing the beauty that surrounds them. They can also use their photos as a way to express their emotions and tell their stories, creating a visual diary of their experiences that they can look back on for years to come. Whether it's capturing the vibrant colors of a blooming flower, the delicate wings of a butterfly, or the playful antics of a squirrel, garden photography is a wonderful way for kids to express themselves and find joy in the world around them.

5.1. THE HEALING POWER OF NATURE: HOW NATURE CAN NURTURE AND RESTORE OUR EMOTIONAL WELL-BEING

Parents, have you considered the healing power of nature for your child's emotional and behavioral well-being? Spending time in nature is a wonderful form of art therapy that can have a positive impact on children. Nature offers a peaceful and calming environment that can help reduce stress and promote relaxation.

There are many ways to incorporate nature into your child's art therapy treatment plan. For example, you can take them on a nature walk in a nearby park or encourage them to create art inspired by nature using materials found in their surroundings, such as leaves, flowers, or twigs. This can help them feel more connected to nature and promote emotional regulation and healthy behaviors.

In today's fast-paced world, it's important to take time to slow down and appreciate the beauty of nature. By incorporating nature into your child's art therapy, you can provide them with a peaceful and calming environment to help regulate their emotions and behaviors.

There are a plethora of enjoyable and inventive methods to integrate the natural world into your child's therapeutic regimen. One example is taking your child on outdoor strolls, which can be conducted in any location and at any time. Even a brief stint spent outside in nature can aid in reducing stress and boosting one's mood. Additional activities involving nature that may benefit your child's emotional and behavioral health include gardening, bird watching, frolicking in the sprinklers, paying a visit to a petting zoo, exploring hiking paths, and fishing. These pursuits can provide your child with a sense of serenity and foster a greater connection with nature.

If venturing outside isn't feasible, you can still bring the natural world into your home. Contemplate keeping greenery indoors, affixing wall stickers with nature themes, or playing recorded nature sounds to establish a soothing ambiance. Nature can also be used as a tool for relaxation. Guided nature meditation and progressive muscle relaxation techniques both use nature sounds to help relax the mind and body.

Finally, consider giving your child nature-based gifts, such as pet rocks, plants, or a nature-themed book. These gifts can help your child feel more connected to the natural world and promote emotional regulation and healthy behaviors. Incorporating nature into your child's emotional and behavioral therapy plan can have a powerful impact on their well-being.

5.2. GARDEN ART THERAPY: CREATING A PERSONAL GARDEN SPACE FOR REFLECTION AND CREATIVITY

If you're looking for a creative way to encourage your child's emotional and behavioral well-being, consider the therapeutic benefits of creating a personal garden. Gardening has been shown to promote relaxation and reduce stress and anxiety, making it a great form of therapy for children.

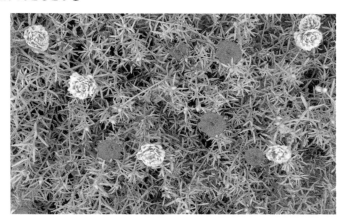

Here are some creative and unique ideas to help your child create a personal garden space for reflection and creativity:

Fairy Garden: Create a miniature enchanted world with a fairy garden. Encourage your child to create a small space filled with houses, bridges and other magical elements. They can add plants and flowers to create a playful and peaceful atmosphere.

Sensory Garden: A sensory garden is designed to stimulate the senses, making it a great therapeutic tool for children with sensory processing difficulties. Add plants with different textures, scents and colors and encourage your child to touch, smell and even taste the plants.

Zen Garden: A Zen garden is a minimalist garden that promotes relaxation and mindfulness. Encourage your child to create a small space filled with miniature rocks, sand, and rakes. They can use the rake to create patterns in the sand, promoting relaxation and concentration.

Vegetable garden: Planting and maintaining a vegetable garden can be a great way to encourage healthy eating habits and a sense of accomplishment. Encourage your child to choose their favorite vegetables and herbs to grow and teach them about plant care.

Flower Garden: A flower garden is a beautiful and calming place that can encourage relaxation and creativity. Encourage your child to choose their favorite flowers and colors and plant them in a designated spot. You can also add decorative elements like wind chimes or garden ornaments.

Butterfly Garden: Create a space that attracts butterflies by planting a variety of nectar plants and providing a place for them to lay their eggs. Your child can observe butterflies and learn about their life cycle, encouraging a sense of wonder and curiosity.

Rock Garden: A rock garden is a low-maintenance, visually appealing space that can encourage relaxation and creativity. Encourage your child to choose their favorite bricks and arrange them in a pattern or design. You can also add plants or other decorative elements to create a unique and calming space. Creating a personal garden space can be a fun and therapeutic activity for children. Encourage your child to choose a garden theme that appeals to him and help him gather the necessary materials. This activity not only encourages creativity and thinking, but can also be a great way to spend time together.

5.3. NATURE CRAFTS: EXPLORING AND EXPRESSING EMOTIONS THROUGH NATURAL MATERIALS

Nature crafting is a type of art therapy that involves using materials found in nature to create art. This includes using plants, soil, and even the sounds in the environment. It is a creative way to engage with nature, reduce stress, and enhance mindfulness.

Nature crafting is beneficial for all ages and can be adapted to work with very young children. It is an excellent way to get children off their screens and into the natural world. The benefits of nature crafting include developing creativity, improving fine motor skills, increasing awareness of nature, and reducing stress and anxiety.

There are many types of nature crafts that children can engage in. One example is leaf and bark rubbings, which involves placing plants between a piece of paper and a hard surface and gently coloring over them to bring out the details. Another example is nature tracings, where children trace the outlines of natural objects such as leaves and flowers onto paper. Nature mosaics or collages involve collecting and pressing different parts of plants and arranging them on a sturdy background. Soil painting is another creative activity where children mix different types of soil with water to create unique paintings in shades of brown. Tape bracelets involve creating a bracelet with tape and covering it with natural objects to create a fun and wearable accessory.

Exploring plant pigments is a simple activity that involves collecting colorful natural objects such as flower petals and rubbing them against a piece of paper to leave their pigment behind. This results in a very pretty and unique artwork.

5.4. CAPTURING YOUR EMOTIONS

Photography can be a powerful tool for children to express and process their emotions. Capturing images allows children to explore their feelings and experiences and convey them in a visual form. Photography can be a form of art therapy, encouraging self-expression, self-awareness and self-discovery.

Here are some ways photography can help children capture their emotions:

Visual Storytelling: Photography allows children to tell a story with pictures. By taking photos of different things that represent their emotions or experiences, they can create a visual story that helps them process and communicate their feelings.

Mindfulness and observation: Photography can also help children practice mindfulness and observation. By focusing on their surroundings and taking time to notice details, children can become more present in the moment and develop a deeper appreciation of their surroundings.

Reflection: Reviewing their photos can help children reflect on their experiences and feelings. It can also help them see patterns and issues in their lives, which can lead to greater self-awareness and understanding.

Here are some techniques that parents can recommend to their children when taking photos:

Close-ups: Encourage your child to take close-ups of objects that represent their emotions or experiences. It can help them focus on details and capture the essence of their feelings.

Perspective: Encourage your child to experiment with different perspectives when taking photos. This can include shooting from high or low angles, or using different lenses to achieve different effects.

Light and shadow: Encourage your child to pay attention to how light and shadow affect the mood and atmosphere of their photos. It can help them convey different emotions and experiences through their images.

Experimentation: Encourage your child to experiment with different techniques, such as long exposures, multiple exposures, or editing techniques. This can help them create unique and expressive images that reflect their individual style and creativity.

Photography can be a valuable tool for children to explore and express their emotions. By encouraging your child to experiment with different techniques and approaches, you can help them develop their creativity and self-awareness and use photography as a form of art therapy.

CONCLUSION

Unlock the boundless potential of your child's inner artist with the transformative power of art therapy! This comprehensive workbook is your ultimate guide to help your child aged 9-12 boost their emotional resilience, improve their behavior, and enhance their social and communication skills. By tapping into the therapeutic benefits of creative expression, your child can discover new depths of self-awareness and empowerment, all from the comfort of your own home. Through an array of fun and engaging art activities, this workbook provides a secure and encouraging environment for your child to delve into their emotions and ideas, and unleash their artistic potential in ways they may have never imagined. With this invaluable tool at your fingertips, you can help your child overcome anxiety, low self-esteem, and communication challenges, and unlock the key to a brighter and more expressive future. So, get ready to embark on an unforgettable journey of self-discovery with your child, and let the power of art therapy work its magic!

Printed in Great Britain
by Amazon

46565980R00044